EVERYTHING SPORTS

EVERYTHING BASKETBALL

LUKE HANLON

SportsZone
An Imprint of Abdo Publishing
abdobooks.com

abdobooks.com

Published by Abdo Publishing, a division of ABDO, PO Box 398166, Minneapolis, Minnesota 55439.

Printed in the United States of America, North Mankato, Minnesota.
052024
092024

THIS BOOK CONTAINS RECYCLED MATERIALS

Cover Photos: Eric Gay/AP Images, front (Victor Wembanyama); Jeff Chiu/AP Images, front (Anthony Edwards); Shutterstock Images, front (background), back
Interior Photos: Frank Gunn/The Canadian Press/AP Images, 4–5, 6–7; AP Images, 8–9, 12–13; John Greim/LightRocket/Getty Images, 10; Blanchard Harper/Wisconsin Historical Society/Archive Photos/Getty Images, 14–15; Mike Powell/Getty Images Sport/Getty Images, 17; Ronald Martinez/Allsport/Getty Images Sport/Getty Images, 18–19; Focus on Sport/Getty Images, 20–21; Al Messerschmidt/AP Images, 22–23; Allen J. Schaben/Los Angeles Times/Getty Images, 24; Ronald Martinez/Getty Images Sport/Getty Images, 27; Steve Marcus/Getty Images Sport/Getty Images, 28; Bob Riha Jr./Archive Photos/Getty Images, 30–31; Rich Clarkson/NCAA Photos/Getty Images, 32–33; Chris Graythen/Getty Images Sport/Getty Images, 34–35; Streeter Lecka/Getty Images Sport/Getty Images, 36–37; Gerry Broome/AP Images, 39; Ron Jenkins/Getty Images Sport/Getty Images, 40–41; John Gaps III/AP Images, 43; Andy Lyons/Getty Images Sport/Getty Images, 44; Aaron Ontiveroz/Denver Post/Getty Images, 46–47; Rich Pedroncelli/AP Images, 49; Ezra Shaw/Getty Images Sport/Getty Images, 50–51, 52–53; Maddie Meyer/Getty Images Sport/Getty Images, 54–55; Eric Risberg/AP Images, 57; Christian Peterson/Getty Images Sport/Getty Images, 59; Adam Hunger/AP Images, 60–61

Editor: Charlie Beattie
Series Designer: Karli Kruse

Library of Congress Control Number: 2023949393
Publisher's Cataloging-in-Publication Data
Names: Hanlon, Luke, author.
Title: Everything basketball / by Luke Hanlon
Description: Minneapolis, Minnesota: Abdo Publishing, 2025 | Series: Everything sports | Includes online resources and index.
Identifiers: ISBN 9781098293567 (lib. bdg.) | ISBN 9798384912835 (ebook)
Subjects: LCSH: Basketball--Juvenile literature. | Basketball teams--Juvenile literature. | Basketball players--Juvenile literature. | Basketball injuries--Juvenile literature. | Basketball fans--Juvenile literature. | Basketball coaches--Juvenile literature. | Basketball managers--Juvenile literature. | Sports--Juvenile literature. | Basketball--History--Juvenile literature. | Basketball--Records--Juvenile literature.
Classification: DDC 796.323--dc23

TABLE OF CONTENTS

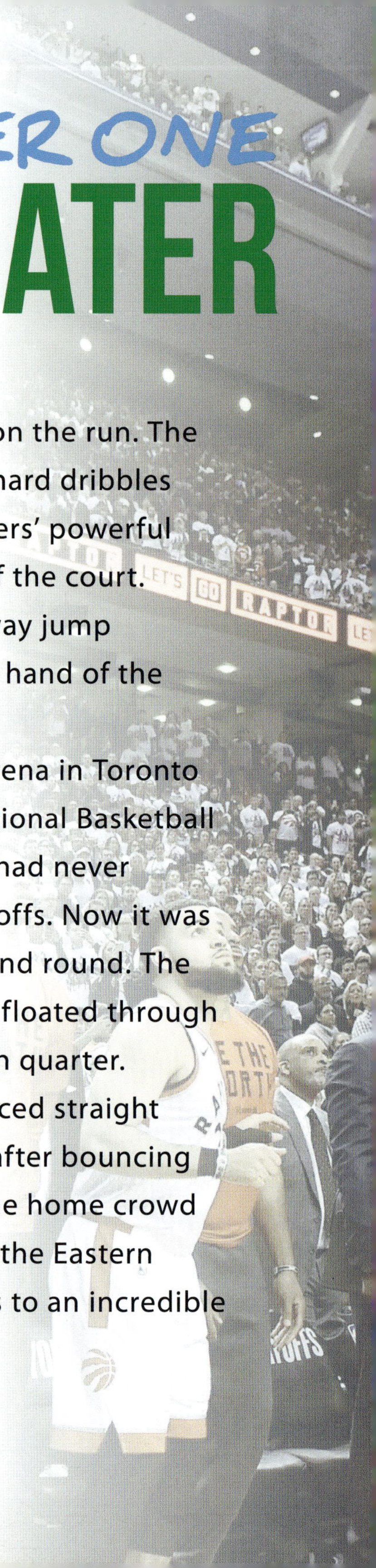

CHAPTER ONE

BUZZER-BEATER

Kawhi Leonard caught the inbounds pass on the run. The Toronto Raptors' forward then took four hard dribbles to his right. Joel Embiid, the Philadelphia 76ers' powerful center, chased Leonard to the right corner of the court. Both men rose into the air. Leonard's fadeaway jump shot just barely sailed over the outstretched hand of the 7-foot Embiid.

For a moment, everyone in Scotiabank Arena in Toronto fell silent. The Raptors were in their 24th National Basketball Association (NBA) season. In that time, they had never advanced past the second round of the playoffs. Now it was Game 7 of the 2019 Eastern Conference second round. The score was tied 90–90. And as Leonard's shot floated through the air, the buzzer sounded to end the fourth quarter.

The ball clanked hard off the rim. It bounced straight up and down, hitting the rim again. Finally, after bouncing four times, the ball fell through the hoop. The home crowd erupted in joy. The Raptors were heading to the Eastern Conference finals. And they got there thanks to an incredible buzzer-beater.

Kawhi Leonard's shot against Philadelphia was just the ninth series-ending buzzer-beater since the NBA playoffs began in 1947.

Teams combine to make dozens of baskets in any given basketball game. Few moments are as thrilling as a basket that decides the game as time expires. These shots are known as buzzer-beaters. Anticipation builds before the play even starts. The offensive team usually draws up a play to get the ball into the hands of its best scorer. Then in a split second, the outcome of the game is decided by a make or a miss. While everyone waits for that outcome, the sound of the buzzer serves as a noisy reminder of the stakes. Fans and teammates may get a moment of pure joy if their star player comes through in the clutch. Or they may feel agony if the shot is off the mark. Either way, the buzzer beater is sure to make for a memorable finish. It is just one of the many exciting plays that can happen on a basketball court.

BACK-TO-BACK

Arike Ogunbowale scored not one but two iconic buzzer-beaters in 2018. Her Notre Dame team reached that year's Women's Final Four. Ogunbowale's shot with a second left in overtime sent the Fighting Irish past Connecticut and on to the championship game. Two days later, Ogunbowale hit another shot at the buzzer to defeat Mississippi State and secure the national title.

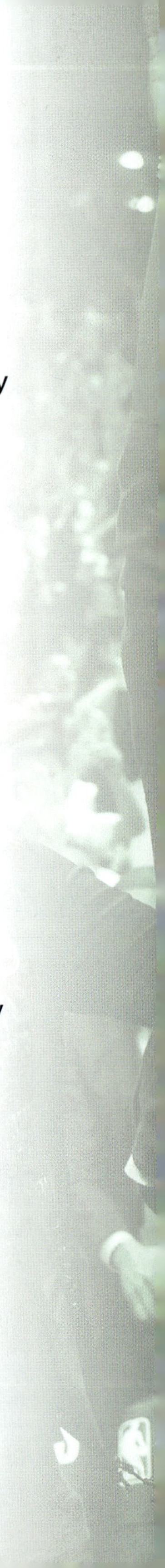

Leonard's shot sent the Toronto Raptors to the Eastern Conference finals on their way to eventually winning the 2019 NBA championship.

CHAPTER TWO

HUMBLE BEGINNINGS

James Naismith faced a problem. The male students at the International Young Men's Christian Association (YMCA) Training School in Springfield, Massachusetts played outdoor sports in the fall and spring. But it was too cold to play outside in the winter. Naismith was a physical education teacher at the school. He could see that his students were bored with their repetitive exercises in the gym. So in 1891, he created a new indoor competition.

Naismith's new game involved tossing a soccer ball into an elevated goal. The school's janitor provided two peach baskets to use as the goals. Naismith nailed them onto the rails of a balcony in the gym that were 10 feet (3 m) above the ground. Little did he know at the time, but Naismith had created a sport that eventually would be played by millions of people around the world.

James Naismith invented basketball in Springfield, Massachusetts, and later went on to coach at the University of Kansas.

The Naismith Memorial Basketball Hall of Fame is in Springfield, Massachusetts, where James Naismith invented the sport.

Early versions of basketball looked quite different from today's game. At first, a successful shot landed in the basket and stayed there. A person standing on each side of the balcony had to pop the ball out of the basket to put it back into play. After a few years of playing this way, the bottoms of the baskets were cut out. This allowed play to restart more quickly.

LITERAL NAME

In 1892, one of James Naismith's students asked what he was going to call his new game. The student suggested calling it "Naismith ball." Naismith felt the game wouldn't be popular with a name like that. The student then asked, "Why not call it basket ball?" After all, the sport was shooting a ball into a basket. Naismith loved the name, and it stuck, although it would eventually become one word: basketball.

There were a few other key differences in Naismith's original game. No dribbling was allowed. In fact, players couldn't move when they had possession of the ball. They had to pass to move it up the court. Also, instead of five players per team, there were nine on each side.

The game was an instant hit among Naismith's students. In January 1892, Springfield College's school magazine published the rules of basketball. Soon, high schools and colleges began introducing their students to the new game.

In 1893, the first women began playing basketball. That same year, colleges started to organize games against local YMCAs. The first official game between two men's college teams took place in 1895 in Minnesota. Two years later, teams began playing with five players on the court at a time. By 1900, colleges around the United States had men's basketball teams. Various leagues and tournaments were founded in the early 1900s. In 1939, the National Collegiate Athletic Association (NCAA) held its first tournament to crown a men's college basketball champion.

The women's game, though, didn't take off until much later. Many people looked down on women's sports. Women's college basketball didn't truly gain support until the 1970s.

Meanwhile, a handful of professional men's leagues came and went in the early 1900s. The National Basketball League (NBL) started in 1937. The NBL was the country's most popular basketball league until the Basketball Association of America (BAA) began play in 1946. Unlike the NBL, the BAA based its teams in major cities such as New York and Boston. The two leagues eventually merged in 1949, forming the NBA. Naismith's gym class game was now a major sport.

George Mikan (99), one of the NBA's first superstars, goes up for a layup while playing for the Minneapolis Lakers in 1949.

CHAPTER THREE

WOMEN IN THE GAME

Less than a year after James Naismith invented basketball, Senda Berenson became interested in the sport. Like Naismith, Berenson was a physical education teacher looking to encourage her students to stay active during the winter. Berenson worked at the all-female Smith College in Northampton, Massachusetts. She began teaching basketball to her class in 1892.

By March 1893, Berenson had organized the first women's basketball game. While she was inspired by Naismith's original idea, her version had some different rules. There were six players per team, not nine. And the court was divided into three sections, with players not allowed to leave their section of the court.

Women's basketball players at the University of Wisconsin prepare to start a game with a tip-off in the early 1900s.

SIX-ON-SIX

For years, alternate girls' basketball rules lived on in some states. In one version of the game, each team featured six players. Three forwards played on one half of the court, and three guards played on the other half. The players couldn't cross the half-court line, so the guards played defense and the forwards played offense. When Title IX passed, most states stopped using this format. However, Oklahoma played this way until 1985.

Though women enjoyed the sport, their opportunities were limited compared to men. Competitive sports were thought to be too strenuous for women to play. Berenson was against using the game for competition. Instead, she intended for women to play basketball only to stay in good physical shape. As a result, she and other female physical education teachers at the time tried to limit travel, awards, and media attention for the sport.

The concerns about women playing basketball also affected the rules of the game. Until 1938, the court remained divided into three sections. The current format of five players on each team playing on the entire court didn't become official until 1971.

The biggest advancement for women's basketball came in 1972. That year, the United States passed Title IX. The law was designed to stop gender discrimination in schools funded by the US government. Though sports were not the

High-scoring forward Cheryl Miller led the University of Southern California (USC) Trojans to NCAA titles in 1983 and 1984.

focus of Title IX, the law had a massive impact on girls' and women's sports. Schools had to create more opportunities for girls to play sports, similar to those for boys. As a result, participation in girls' sports grew dramatically. Few sports benefited as much as basketball. Many colleges formed women's teams after Title IX passed. By the 1981–82 season, the NCAA had taken control of the women's game. Now both men and women played under the same organization.

The next step was creating professional opportunities for women. The Women's Professional Basketball League started in 1978. However, it lasted only three seasons. That became a trend for women's pro basketball leagues in the United States. Most only lasted a couple of years. But women's basketball rode a new wave of popularity that hit during the 1996 Summer Olympics in Atlanta. Led by stars such as Lisa Leslie, Rebecca Lobo, and Sheryl Swoopes, Team USA won gold and caught the attention of fans across the country.

The NBA had noticed how popular the women's game was becoming. In 1997, eight NBA teams helped launch the Women's National Basketball Association (WNBA). The new league signed Leslie, Lobo, Swoopes, and many other stars. Those pioneers helped start the league, and many superstars over the years helped it thrive.

Cynthia Cooper and the Houston Comets were the WNBA's first dynasty. The team won the league's first four championships.

CHAPTER FOUR

ICONIC MEN'S PLAYERS

Throughout the history of the NBA, certain players have defined entire eras. The league had stars before Bill Russell debuted in 1956. But no player was as successful as the Boston Celtics big man. The 6-foot-10 center was such a dominant defender and rebounder that he could shut down opposing offenses almost by himself. His leadership, though, might have been his greatest skill. Russell always put team success over his own stats. The center led the Celtics to 11 NBA championships in 13 seasons. Two came while he was also serving as the team's coach in the late 1960s.

Magic Johnson and Larry Bird didn't just define their teams, but rather the entire league. They first squared off in the 1979 NCAA title game. The pair then moved on to the NBA. Johnson went to the Los Angeles Lakers while Bird played for the Celtics. Some fans were drawn to Johnson, the flashy point guard. Others preferred the well-rounded Bird,

The battles between Bill Russell (6) and fellow legendary center Wilt Chamberlain (13) in the 1960s were one of the NBA's main attractions.

a forward. Fans couldn't get enough of their rivalry. The two appeared in commercials together. Their games were often aired on national television. And the NBA Finals featured at least one of the two stars every year of the 1980s.

Their success helped the NBA reach a new level of popularity. Then Michael Jordan came and supercharged it. The shooting guard was a star right away when the Chicago Bulls drafted him in 1984. But his popularity soared in the 1990s as he led the Bulls to six championships. Jordan was NBA Finals Most Valuable Player (MVP) each time. His ability to come through in clutch moments captivated fans. And he took player marketing to new heights. Jordan had his own signature shoes from Nike. He also appeared in dozens of commercials. His superstardom turned Bulls games into must-see television events.

SCORING MACHINE

Kareem Abdul-Jabbar had already won an NBA championship with the Milwaukee Bucks when the Lakers traded for him in 1975. Magic Johnson later joined the 7-foot-2 center, and the duo won five NBA titles together. Abdul-Jabbar used his height and touch to score over opponents with ease. He held the NBA all-time scoring record with 38,387 points until LeBron James passed him in 2023.

Michael Jordan won the NBA scoring title 10 times in his 15-year career. He also won five regular-season MVP awards.

LeBron James became the first player in NBA history to score 30,000 points, grab 10,000 rebounds, and dish out 10,000 assists in his career.

When LeBron James was 17, *Sports Illustrated* magazine put him on its cover. Some experts predicted he could be the next Jordan-like star. The hype made James a household name before he even entered the NBA with his hometown Cleveland Cavaliers as an 18-year-old in 2003. Somehow, he lived up to that hype.

The 6-foot, 9-inch, 250-pound forward has used his amazing athleticism to dominate the NBA for more than 20 years. James also led three different teams to NBA titles. He won two with the Miami Heat in the early 2010s. Then he went back to his native Cleveland and helped the Cavaliers win their first championship in team history. In 2020, James took the Lakers to the franchise's record-tying 17th title.

Like Jordan, James had his own Nike shoes and plenty of endorsement deals. Debates have raged on about who was the better player. However, no one can debate that both superstars helped the NBA become even more popular.

CHAPTER FIVE

ICONIC WOMEN'S PLAYERS

The first WNBA commercial featured Lisa Leslie, Rebecca Lobo, and Sheryl Swoopes. All three had helped the US women's team win an Olympic gold medal in 1996. And all would go on to set a foundation for the new league to grow. However, the league's biggest early star was not on that Olympic team.

Cynthia Cooper had led the USC Trojans to NCAA titles in 1983 and 1984. Then she had to wait for more than a decade to play professional basketball in the United States. When the WNBA began in 1997, she got her opportunity. The high-scoring guard played four full seasons with the Houston Comets, where she teamed up with Swoopes. The team won WNBA championships all four years. And Cooper won the WNBA Finals MVP Award each time.

Eventually, Leslie took over as the league's dominant player. Her strong play at both ends of the court led her Los Angeles Sparks to championships in 2001 and 2002.

And the 6-foot-5 center made history in 2002 when she became the first player to dunk in a WNBA game. In addition to dominating on the court, Leslie found fame off the floor. She appeared in several commercials and was a successful model. Leslie's stardom showed future players how they could use their platform to help grow the league.

Sheryl Swoopes was the first women's basketball player to have her own signature shoe.

No WNBA player has scored with as much ease as Diana Taurasi. Going into the 2024 WNBA season, Taurasi had 10,108 career points. The next closest player hadn't even

In her first six WNBA seasons, A'ja Wilson was the league's MVP twice, Defensive Player of the Year twice, and an All-Star five times.

topped 7,500. The guard's consistent scoring helped the Phoenix Mercury win three WNBA championships between 2007 and 2014. Taurasi was named the Finals MVP in two of those wins.

These legends helped inspire future generations of players. In 2023, two of the WNBA's top stars met in that year's league championship. New York Liberty forward Breanna Stewart could create her own shot with ease. She had won her second MVP Award that season. Las Vegas Aces forward A'ja Wilson thought she should have won the award instead. When the two teams met in the Finals, Wilson put her dominant scoring, rebounding, and defense on display. She won the Finals MVP Award and led the Aces to their second straight championship. Both Stewart and Wilson built on what stars before them had done to take the WNBA to a new level.

ALL SHE DOES IS WIN

Maya Moore boasted a 150–4 record and won two college national championships at Connecticut. The Minnesota Lynx then selected the forward with the first pick in 2011 WNBA Draft. In her first season, Moore led the long-struggling team to a championship. It was the first of six Finals appearances, and four wins, in seven years for Moore and Minnesota. Moore also won Olympic gold with Team USA in 2012 and 2016.

CHAPTER SIX

DYNASTIES

Throughout its history, the NBA has featured several great dynasties. Since the league began, one team has won at least three championships in every decade except the 1970s. Before the Lakers moved to Los Angeles in the 1960s, they were the Minneapolis Lakers. The team won four titles in five seasons in the late 1940s and early 1950s. The Boston Celtics ruled the 1960s. The Lakers and Celtics controlled the 1980s. Then the Chicago Bulls dominated the 1990s.

The era of dynasties appeared to be over when the NBA introduced a salary cap for the 1984–85 season. The cap put a limit on how much a team could spend on players. It ensured that the richest teams couldn't sign all of the best talent. But teams still found ways to load up on stars.

In 2006, guard Dwyane Wade led the Miami Heat to a championship. Four years later, two of his friends from the 2003 draft class decided to join him. All-Star forwards LeBron James and Chris Bosh linked up with Wade in Miami. All three took less money to play with one another. The team's fans were thrilled to have three likely Hall of Famers

The Boston Celtics and Los Angeles Lakers are the only two NBA franchises that have won at least 10 league championships.

UCLA's dynasty of the 1960s and 1970s was led by head coach John Wooden. Many consider him the greatest college basketball coach of all time.

on the roster. However, outside of Miami many fans despised the new "super team." The Heat embraced being villains. In four years together, the trio reached four NBA Finals. In 2012 and 2013, they won.

Dynasties have also had major impacts in college basketball. No team has been as successful as the men's team at the University of California, Los Angeles (UCLA). The Bruins had dominant players such as Kareem Abdul-Jabbar, then known as Lew Alcindor, and Bill Walton in the late 1960s and early 1970s. UCLA won 10 championships in 12 seasons between 1964 and 1975. Since then, only Duke (1991 and 1992) and Florida (2006 and 2007) have repeated as champions.

Immaculata and Delta State each earned a three-peat in the years before the NCAA took over women's basketball in 1982. Before long, Pat Summitt set a new standard in the sport. Tennessee's head coach motivated her talented teams to play up to their potential. Summitt led the Lady Vols to six titles from 1987 to 1998. They also won championships in 2007 and 2008 under Summitt.

Tennessee's success inspired other programs. Like Summitt, Connecticut head coach Geno Auriemma demanded greatness from his players. In 1995, they delivered perfection. The Huskies defeated Tennessee in that

GOLDEN EXPECTATIONS

Perhaps no basketball team has been as dominant as the US women's national team. The team won its 55th consecutive Olympic game in the gold-medal contest against Japan at the Tokyo Olympics in 2021. That streak had started at the 1996 Olympic Games in Atlanta.

year's championship game to finish off just the second undefeated season in NCAA women's basketball history.

The budding rivalry between the two schools soon captivated fans. Connecticut beat Tennessee in the 2000, 2003, and 2004 title games. Between 1987 and 2016, the two schools won a combined total of 19 titles. The success of each program drove the other to become better. And their rivalry brought new attention to the sport.

At one point between 2014 and 2017, Geno Auriemma's Connecticut Huskies won 111 games in a row.

CHAPTER SEVEN

MARCH MADNESS

For three weeks every spring, sports fans across the United States turn their attention to college basketball. The sport uses single-elimination tournaments to crown the men's and women's winners. This format creates a mix of unpredictability and excitement that has become known as March Madness.

The first men's NCAA Tournament was held in 1939 and featured eight teams. The tournament eventually expanded to 64 teams in 1985, with four regions of teams seeded 1 to 16. Favorites earn higher seeds, but that doesn't mean they always win.

The unexpectedness of March Madness was on full display in 1985. Georgetown had won the 1984 title. Behind dominant senior center Patrick Ewing, the top-seeded

Duke men's coach Mike Krzyzewski helped his team cut down the nets after winning the 2015 NCAA Tournament. The winner cutting the nets down is one of the tournament's many traditions.

Hoyas were favored to repeat. After five mostly comfortable wins, all Georgetown needed to do was beat the upstart Villanova Wildcats in the championship game. Instead, the No. 8-seeded Wildcats stunned the Hoyas—and the country—by making 79 percent of their shots in a massive upset. Villanova became the lowest seed to win the tournament.

Lower seeds are less likely to win. But upsets are a feature of March Madness. And occasionally, they're big. In the 1998 women's tournament, Harvard became the first No. 16 seed to beat a No. 1 when it toppled Stanford. Two teams seeded 15th beat No. 2 seeds in the 2012 men's tournament. Six years later a No. 16 beat a No. 1 on the men's side. That year, the University of Maryland, Baltimore County (UMBC) shocked top-seeded Virginia in the first round.

Another feature of March Madness is crazy finishes. As the tournament

TITLE-WINNING SLAM

The 1983 men's national championship game was tied with three seconds left. North Carolina State guard Dereck Whittenburg launched a shot from near half-court. The ball fell short of the basket. But teammate Lorenzo Charles caught it and dunked it just before time expired to beat Houston. North Carolina State head coach Jim Valvano couldn't contain his excitement. He ran around the court looking for a player to hug.

Upsets like UMBC's shocking win over Virginia in 2018 have helped the NCAA Tournaments become popular with fans.

goes on and the stakes get higher, legends are born from iconic moments. In the 1992 men's tournament, top-seeded Duke trailed No. 2 seed Kentucky 103–102 with 2.1 seconds left in overtime. Even worse, the Blue Devils needed to go the length of the floor. Duke forward Grant Hill heaved a one-handed pass to teammate Christian Laettner, who caught it at the free-throw line with his back to the basket. Laettner took one dribble, then hit a turnaround jump shot at the buzzer to send Duke to the Final Four. Laettner and Duke went on to their second straight national championship that year.

Some of the most memorable moments in March Madness occur when a dramatic upset takes place. Mississippi State was a No. 2 seed in the 2017 women's tournament, and it made a run to the Final Four. A No. 2 seed usually isn't a big underdog, but the Bulldogs were facing a Connecticut team that had won 111 games in a row. Mississippi State guard Morgan William hit a buzzer-beater in overtime to end the longest winning streak in college basketball history.

Mississippi State's Morgan William, *right*, was mobbed by teammates after her buzzer-beater took down Connecticut in the 2017 national semifinals.

CHAPTER EIGHT

AROUND THE GLOBE

Though basketball started in the United States, it has international roots. James Naismith was born in Canada, and the original class that he taught basketball to featured multiple international students. Many of them then brought the game to their home countries. Basketball became popular enough around the world that a men's tournament was added to the 1936 Olympics.

For years, the United States sent amateur players to the Olympics. That changed at the 1992 Games in Barcelona, Spain. For the first time, NBA players were allowed to represent Team USA in the Olympics. And the stars showed up in a big way. Michael Jordan, Magic Johnson, and Larry Bird were among the biggest names. This squad became known as the Dream Team. Eleven of the 12 players were eventually inducted into the Hall of Fame, as was the team itself.

The team steamrolled its way to the gold medal. And it became a global sensation in the process. Members of other teams were starstruck by the US players. And fans around the world were amazed to see the NBA's superstars for the first time.

In the years after the 1992 Olympics, basketball's popularity exploded around the world. The International Basketball Federation estimates that 450 million people now play basketball. That makes it one of the most played sports

The 1992 Dream Team beat its Olympic opponents by an average of 44 points per game.

Hakeem Olajuwon, *left*, of Nigeria became the first foreign player to win NBA MVP when he took home the award after the 1993–94 season.

in the world. This growth in participation eventually led to a surge in international players making the NBA. At the start of the 1991–92 NBA season, the league had 23 international players from 18 countries. At the start of the 2023–24 season, 125 international players represented 40 countries and territories. Many of the international stars have said they were inspired by the Dream Team.

AUSTRALIAN SENSATION

The WNBA has not seen the same surge of international players as the NBA. But multiple international stars have made a big impact on the league. None have been more significant than Lauren Jackson. The 6-foot-6 Australian was the top pick in the WNBA Draft in 2001. Jackson went on to win three MVP Awards and two WNBA titles with the Seattle Storm.

Many of the modern NBA's top stars were born outside of the United States. Greece's Giannis Antetokounmpo uses his overpowering athleticism to dominate opponents. Serbian center Nikola Jokić is one of the best passers the NBA has ever seen. Antetokounmpo and Jokić each won back-to-back MVP Awards from 2019 to 2022. The streak of international MVPs continued in 2023, as Cameroon-born Joel Embiid earned the award. Young superstars such as Slovenia's Luka Dončić, Canada's Shai Gilgeous-Alexander, and France's Victor Wembanyama have taken the NBA by storm as well.

CHAPTER NINE

SUCCESSFUL STRATEGIES

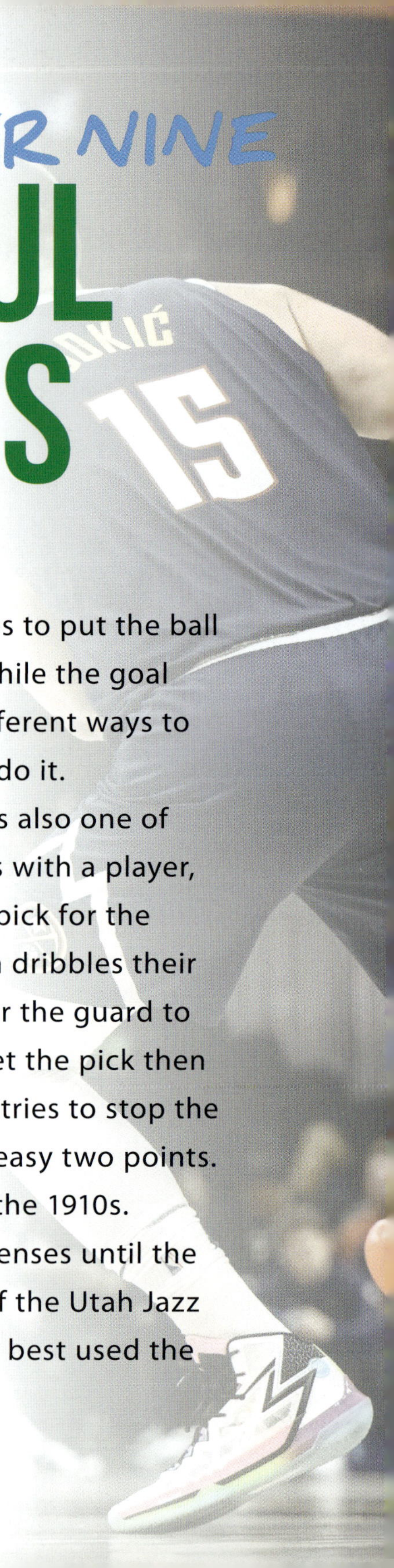

Basketball is a simple game. Each team tries to put the ball through the hoop as often as possible. While the goal is the same for everyone, there are many different ways to score. And teams use different strategies to do it.

One of the simplest offensive strategies is also one of the most effective: the pick-and-roll. It starts with a player, usually a center or forward, coming to set a pick for the ball handler, usually a guard. The guard then dribbles their defender into the pick. That creates space for the guard to shoot or drive. Meanwhile, the player who set the pick then pivots and rolls to the basket. If the defense tries to stop the guard, the pick setter is usually open for an easy two points.

The pick-and-roll has been around since the 1910s. However, it wasn't a main feature of NBA offenses until the 1980s. Jerry Sloan became the head coach of the Utah Jazz in 1988. Sloan wanted to run an offense that best used the

Denver Nuggets forward Nikola Jokić, *left*, sets a screen for teammate Jamal Murray.

skills of point guard John Stockton and power forward Karl Malone. The pick-and-roll worked perfectly for the duo. More often than not, the play ended with Stockton assisting a Malone bucket. Stockton's 15,806 assists are by far the most in NBA history. Malone had scored 36,928 points when he retired in 2004. That was the second-most of any player at the time.

2–3 ZONE

Most college and pro basketball teams run a man-to-man defense, where one player defends a specific opponent. A few teams run zone defenses instead. Most notably, Syracuse men's coach Jim Boeheim ran a 2–3 zone for decades. In the 2–3, two players cover the top of the three-point line. The other three players cover the lane and the two corners of the court. All defenders must move quickly to cover open spaces when the ball is passed around.

Not all strategies are about running plays. Some offensive strategies give players more freedom. When Becky Hammon took over as the Las Vegas Aces head coach in 2022, she installed an offense that showcased the skills of star players A'ja Wilson, Kelsey Plum, and Chelsea Gray. The system focused on pace, space, and sharing the ball.

The Aces had supremely talented offensive players. Playing at a faster pace helped them launch as many shots as possible. Having players stretch beyond the three-point line also gave the Aces' best players more room to operate.

Karl Malone, *right*, and John Stockton were teammates on the Utah Jazz for 18 years.

And sharing the ball with teammates created more open shots for an offense.

These simple instructions worked wonders for the Aces. After Hammon took over as the coach, Las Vegas had the top scoring offense in the WNBA in 2022 and 2023. The Aces' offense led them to championships in both of those seasons.

CHAPTER TEN

THREE-POINT REVOLUTION

Steph Curry made 25 three-pointers in the 2015 NBA Finals. The guard's elite shooting helped lift the Golden State Warriors to their first NBA championship in 40 years. Curry and his teammates were in the middle of a basketball revolution.

The three-point shot wasn't introduced to the NBA until the 1979–80 season. For years after it came into the league, teams rarely used it. In the 1990s and 2000s, sharpshooters Reggie Miller and Ray Allen ushered in a new era of scoring. Steve Kerr was another great shooter. His 45.4 percent shooting from outside was a record when he retired in 2003.

Kerr took over as the Warriors' head coach before the 2014–15 season. It was no coincidence that three-pointers quickly became a main part of the Golden State offense. Golden State hit 883 three-pointers that season. That same year, the Houston Rockets set a new NBA record with 933.

Steph Curry shoots a three-pointer over the outstretched arm of a Cleveland Cavaliers' defender during the 2018 NBA Finals.

Three-point shooting helped the Warriors build a dynasty in the 2010s and 2020s.

Houston's hold on the record didn't last long. The next season, the Warriors hit 1,077. With accurate shooters such as Curry and Klay Thompson, the Warriors reached six NBA Finals from 2015 to 2022 and won four of them.

The 1,077 three-pointers made by the 2015–16 Warriors was an absurd total at the time. Yet in the seven years after, that mark was topped 25 times. The reason teams have started to rely more on the three-pointer is a change in attitude. For years, teams felt the three-pointer was too risky of a shot. They wanted to shoot from as close to the basket as possible. But teams started to figure out that they had almost as good a chance of making three-pointers as they did mid-range jump shots. Therefore, getting the additional point for each made three-pointer was worth the risk of shooting from distance.

A similar revolution took place in women's basketball. Idaho's Taylor Pierce made a record 154 threes during the

THREE-POINT OVERLOAD

Former Houston Rockets general manager Daryl Morey helped start the three-point revolution. Then his Rockets teams in the late 2010s took it to another level. In 2017–18, Houston became the first NBA team to shoot more three-pointers than two-pointers in a season. The Rockets matched that feat again in 2018–19 and 2019–20. No other team in NBA history has shot more threes than twos.

2018–19 season. In 2022–23, Oklahoma's Taylor Robertson made her 498th three-pointer to break the record for the most in a career. Robertson eventually reached 537 three-pointers.

Perhaps no player has showcased how the women's game has changed more than Caitlin Clark. The Iowa guard led the NCAA during the 2022–23 season with 140 three-pointers. But the number of threes she makes isn't what stands out. Clark's average three-point shot that season came 26.1 feet away from the basket. That's four feet behind the three-point line. Those deep shots have been a staple of Curry's game for years, and Clark has brought it over to the women's game.

Though her Iowa team lost to Louisiana State 102–85, Caitlin Clark (22) set an NCAA Tournament championship game record with eight three-pointers in the 2023 final.

CHAPTER ELEVEN

DEFENSIVE EFFORT

LeBron James's Cleveland Cavaliers were battling late in Game 7 of the 2016 NBA Finals. In the game's final moments, Golden State Warriors forward Andre Iguodala picked up a loose ball at his own free-throw line. James and three other Cavaliers were behind him, giving Iguodala a clear line to the basket to break the 89–89 tie. But James streaked the length of the floor. He caught Iguodala at the other end. As the Golden State player tried to lay the ball up, James leapt and pinned it against the backboard. James's relentless defensive effort helped the Cavaliers win their first NBA championship.

James's hustle play demonstrated how defense is just as important to winning as offense. Even if a team scores at will, it's hard to win a game if a team can't stop its opponent.

LeBron James is regarded as one of the greatest basketball players of all time. His incredible dunks, pinpoint passes, and clutch shots are all reasons for that. But his stellar defensive plays stand out, too.

LeBron James's block of Andre Iguodala in the 2016 Finals is one of the NBA's most memorable plays.

Great defense can lead to great offense. Often a turnover or a missed shot leaves the other team with little time to get back on defense. Late in Game 5 of the 2021 NBA Finals, Milwaukee Bucks guard Jrue Holiday stole the ball from Phoenix Suns guard Devin Booker. Once Holiday got control of the ball, the Bucks started a three-on-one fast break. Holiday saw his teammate Giannis Antetokounmpo running hard toward the basket. Antetokounmpo caught Holiday's lob pass in midair. He then slammed it home through contact to finish off an alley-oop and secure a win for the Bucks. Milwaukee went on to win the title in Game 6.

HAPPINESS TO HEARTBREAK

The Northern Iowa men's basketball team experienced both sides of dramatic plays during the 2016 NCAA Tournament. In the Panthers' first-round game against Texas, Paul Jesperson hit a half-court buzzer-beater to pull off the upset. In the next round, the Panthers led Texas A&M by 12 with 44 seconds left. Then A&M's pressure defense forced numerous turnovers down the stretch. Northern Iowa blew the lead and lost in overtime.

Teams with the lead late in games are often put under pressure. In these situations, taking care of the ball is the main priority. But if a team gets overwhelmed by the defensive pressure, chaos can take over.

Jrue Holiday's steal in Game 5 of the 2021 NBA Finals led to a highlight-reel dunk for teammate Giannis Antetokounmpo (34).

In a 2019 WNBA elimination playoff game, the Chicago Sky led the Las Vegas Aces 92–90 with 10 seconds left. Chicago guard Courtney Vandersloot was trying to dribble out the clock when she was trapped by a double-team in the backcourt. Vandersloot threw a wild pass over the pressure, which was picked off by Las Vegas' Dearica Hamby. The Aces' forward was just on her own side of half-court. Not realizing that she still had eight seconds to play, Hamby took three steps and heaved up a desperation three-pointer from 38 feet. The shot splashed through the hoop with 4.8 seconds left on the clock. Hamby's amazing steal and heave held up as the winning shot for the Aces.

MASTERS OF DEFENSE

Many great players have been known more for defense than offense. Shot-swatting centers Dikembe Mutombo and Ben Wallace each won the NBA's Defensive Player of the Year Award four times in their careers. But no one starred on defense more than the WNBA's Tamika Catchings. The Indiana Fever forward won her league's top defensive award five times between 2005 and 2012.

Tamika Catchings (24) had 1,074 steals and 385 blocked shots during her 15-year WNBA career.

GLOSSARY

amateur

A person who plays a sport without getting paid.

assists

Passes that lead directly to a basket.

clutch

An important or pressure-packed situation.

draft

A system that allows teams to acquire new players coming into a league.

dynasty

A team that has an extended period of success, usually winning multiple championships in the process.

endorsement

A deal in which an athlete promotes a company in exchange for the company's products or money.

fast break

Move the ball up the floor quickly.

favorites

The people or teams that are expected to win.

general manager

An executive who runs a team and is responsible for finding and signing players.

merged

Joined with another to create something new, such as a company, a team, or a league.

pick

When an offensive player legally blocks the path of a defender to open up a teammate for a shot or a pass.

underdog

The person or team that is not expected to win.

upset

An unexpected victory by a supposedly weaker team or player.

MORE INFORMATION

Books

Giedd, Steph. *Basketball Strategies*. Abdo, 2024.

Hoehn, Jim. *WNBA*. Abdo, 2021.

Kjartan Atli Kjartansson. *Stars of the NBA*. Abbeville Press, 2021.

Online Resources

Booklinks
NONFICTION NETWORK
FREE! ONLINE NONFICTION RESOURCES

To learn more about basketball, please visit **abdobooklinks.com** or scan this QR code. These links are routinely monitored and updated to provide the most current information available.

INDEX

About the Author

Luke Hanlon is a sportswriter and editor based in Minneapolis. He grew up playing basketball and still constantly watches and attends NBA, WNBA, and college basketball games.